MEDITATIONS FOR PEOPLE IN CRISIS

Crisis and suffering are inevitable. But there is a power deep within each one of us which enlightens our soul and vigors our mind.

MEDITATIONS for People in Crisis

Selected from the notebooks of

PAUL BRUNTON

Edited by

SAM & LESLIE COHEN

New Age Books

ISBN: 978-81-7822-341-4

First Indian Edition: Delhi, 2009

Originally published in English in the USA.

This edition published by arrangement with Paul Brunton Philosophic Foundation 4936 NYS Route 414, Burdett, NY 14818 USA

Published by
NEW AGE BOOKS
A-44 Naraina Phase-I
New Delhi-110 028 (INDIA)
Email: nab@vsnl.in
Website: www.newagebooksindia.com

For Sale in South-East Asia Only

Printed in India
at Shri Jainendra Press
A-45 Naraina Phase-I, New Delhi-110 028

CONTENTS

INTRODUCTION

No one can avoid crisis and suffering. For Sam, thirty years of human service and community work have made that abundantly clear. But though we're never really ready when crisis comes, help is always within reach.

When the latest crisis in our lives hit, we felt very grateful to have Paul Brunton's *Notebooks*. In hospital beds or sitting in lounge chairs as chemotherapy dripped into Leslie's veins, we pored over thousands of passages from these writings. The reading buoyed our spirits, rekindling our faith, and in the process this little book came to be.

We hope the passages selected here will help others amidst life's trials and tribulations, as they have helped us.

Leslie and Sam Cohen
Lodi, New York
April 1996

PAUL BRUNTON

1

CAST YOUR BURDEN

There is peace beneath life's pain and peace at the end of its pain.

Even when a situation becomes quite critical, a here-and-now matter, do not give way to panic. The first move after the first shock should be to restore and maintain calm, the second to consider what you are to do—a question for which you should look not only to thinking for an answer but also to intuition.

Whenever an emergency arises wherein you require help, guidance, protection, or inspiration, turn the thought away from self-power and bring it humbly to the feet of the higher power in prayer.

If you can give up your fears and anxieties to the higher self, because you are convinced that it is better able to manage your problems than the egoistic self, because you believe in trusting to its wisdom rather than to your own foolishness, yet do not evade the lessons implicit in those problems, your surrender becomes an act of strength, not of weakness.

Acceptance of suffering is sometimes a key to the way out of it. The greater the suffering, the greater are the possibilities of Peace succeeding it—provided that the lessons to be learned from it have been correctly interpreted and actively applied to daily life.

✽ ✽ ✽

In times of terrible danger, stick to your faith in the divine power as a protective talisman. Whenever you are in difficulty, drop all fear and trouble temporarily from your mind and imagine yourself handing them over to your higher Self, thereby surrendering yourself to its will, help, and protection.

✽ ✽ ✽

Look your sorrows and troubles, your cares and burdens, in the face. Do not deny them. But do not attach to them the interpretations which are commonly attached to them. Instead of lamenting your ill-fate, seek out the reasons why they particularly are present in your life. Instead of sinking into melancholy, remember that you are more than the ego, and refuse to let go of the peace that is behind and above it.

✽ ✽ ✽

Never give yourself up to despair, although you may give yourself up in hard situations to gravest reflection and deepest resignation.

✽ ✽ ✽

If only you heed its intuitive message, the higher self will not fail you. You will make your way to true balanced sanity and deep inner calm. Without searching for others, knowing that in yourself God's representative resides and that this can give the right kind of help, depend for self-reliance on an ever-presence.

✤ ✤ ✤

The innermost being of humanity, the mysterious Overself, links each of us with God. It does not change with time nor die with the years. It is eternal.

✤ ✤ ✤

The World-Mind [God] cannot be separated from any point of the world. It is present in every point, every creature, now, at this very moment. There is no need for anyone to think oneself cut off or apart or remote from this divine source of one's own being. This is just as true in your sorrowful hours as in your joyful ones.

✤ ✤ ✤

When confronted by turmoil, remember to remain calm. When in the presence of ugliness, think of beauty. When others show forth their animality and brutality, show forth spiritual refinement and gentleness. Above all, when all around seems dark and hopeless, remember that nothing can extinguish the Overself's light and that it will shine again as surely as spring follows winter.

✤ ✤ ✤

There is peace *behind* the tumult, goodness *behind* the evil, happiness *behind* the agony.

✤ ✤ ✤

When life in the world becomes so formidable or so frightening that in desperation or bewilderment, panic or mental unbalance, the idea of suicide seems the only way out, then the time has come to cast your burden on the Higher Power.

* * *

There are certain rare moments when intense sorrow or profound bereavement makes you sick at heart. It is then that desires temporarily lose their force, possessions their worth, and even existence itself its reality. You seem to stand outside the busy world whose figures flit to and fro like the shadowy characters on a cinema screen. Worst of all, perhaps, significance vanishes from human activity, which becomes a useless tragi-comedy, a going everywhere and arriving nowhere, an insane playing of instruments from which no music issues forth, a vanity of all the vanities. It is then, too, that a terrible suicidal urge may enter your blood and you will need all your mental ballast not to make away with yourself. Yet these black moments are intensely precious, for they may set your feet firmly on the higher path. Few realize this whilst all complain. The self-destruction to which you are being urged by such dread experiences of life is not the crude physical act, but something subtle—a suicide of thought, emotion, and will. You are being called indeed, to die to your ego, to take the desires and passions, the greeds and hates out of your life, to learn the art of living in utter independence of externals and in utter dependence on the Overself. And this is that same call which Jesus uttered when he said: "He that loseth his life shall find it." Thus the sorrows of life on earth are but a transient means to an eternal end, a process through which we have to learn how to expand awareness from the person to the Overself.

✤ ✤ ✤

The yearning to free yourself from the limitations of personal destiny and the compulsions of outward circumstance can be gratified only by losing the sense of time.

✤ ✤ ✤

If we concentrate attention only on the miseries and distresses which afflict us, then we have to depend on our own intellect to find a way out of them. If, however, we turn concentration in the opposite direction, that of the Overself, and deposit our troubles there, we gain a fresh source of possible help in dealing with them.

✤ ✤ ✤

However bitter a situation may appear, the accepted prompting of the Overself can bring a sweetness into it; however trying it may be, the same prompting can bring fortitude into it.

✤ ✤ ✤

There is a sense of perfect safety, a sense which particularly and strongly reveals itself at times of danger, crisis, or distress.

* * *

Yes, your guardian angel is always present and always the secret witness and recorder of your thoughts and deeds. Whether you go down into the black depths of hell or ascend to the radiant heights of heaven, you do not walk alone.

* * *

There is a power which inspires the heart, enlightens the mind, and sanctifies human character. It is the power of Grace.

* * *

By grace I mean the manifestation of God's friendliness.

* * *

Its power can carry you through a grave crisis with unfaltering steadiness.

* * *

God may help us, or God's healing may come to us, indirectly. Instead of a miracle happening abruptly we may be led intuitively to the knowledge which, or to the person who, will reveal what we can do to serve or save ourselves. The end result may thus be the same as the miracle, but we shall have guided our lives toward it by our own informed effort.

✠ ✠ ✠

However much we pry into the future we do not come a bit nearer real peace, whereas faithfully seeking and abiding in Overself gradually brings undying light and life.

✠ ✠ ✠

In terrible times of suffering and anxiety it is more necessary than ever to cultivate receptivity to the divine forces within ourselves through spiritual studies and meditation.

✠ ✠ ✠

Because there is a Divine Mind back of the universe, there are Divine Wisdom and Goodness in the universe.

✠ ✠ ✠

The universe of our experience is governed by justice and wisdom, by ultimate goodness and infinite power.

✠ ✠ ✠

With the onset of crisis or stress, trouble or calamity, turn your mind instantly toward the Higher Power. This can be done easily, effortlessly—but only after long self-training and much practice in thought control.

✠ ✠ ✠

This instant and unhesitating turning inward is also an effective method of insulating oneself against the currents of fear, despair, and weakness which misfortune often generates.

* * *

This constant remembrance of the higher self becomes in time like a kind of holy communion.

* * *

By this grace the past's errors may be forgotten so that the present's healing may be accepted. In the joy of this grace, the misery of old mistakes may be banished forever. Do not return to the past—live only in the eternal Now—in its peace, love, wisdom, and strength.

* * *

If suffering brings moods of dejection, it is only fulfilling its intention. This is part of its place in the scheme of things, leading to the awareness that underneath the sweet pleasures of life there is always pain. But thought would present only a half-truth if it stopped there. The other half is much harder to find: it is that underneath the surface sufferings which no one escapes, far deeper down than its counterpart, is a vast harmony, an immense love, an incredible peace, and a universal support.

* * *

If, in the act of falling asleep, you invite the higher self through aspiration, you may one day find that in the act of waking up an inner voice begins to speak to you of high and holy things. And with the voice comes the inspiration, the strength, and the desire to live up to them.

✠ ✠ ✠

There are times when the heart's need to feel peace becomes imperative and when the mind's need of long-range perspectives becomes overwhelming. To yield to these needs is not a cowardly escapism but a sensible re-adjustment.

✠ ✠ ✠

To introduce these calm moments quite deliberately and quite regularly is to introduce strength and depth into one's life.

✠ ✠ ✠

Philosophy today represents a refuge for those suffering from the hatred and strife in the world as well as a source of goodness and wisdom for those who seek to permeate their lives with meaning.

✠ ✠ ✠

For those who properly understand it and faithfully practise it, philosophy stands amid the uncertainties and threats of our time as a secure citadel. In it one finds assurance for heart and mind, and will find safe guidance for one's body.

✠ ✠ ✠

These truths, being everlasting and world-wide, give us shelter in periods of violent storm, provide us with refuge in times of distress, and protect us with prudence in years of smiling fortune.

Memorable are those minutes when we sit in silent adoration of the Overself, knowing it to be none other than our own best self. It is as though we have returned to our true home and rest by its hallowed hearth with a contentment nowhere else to be known. No longer do we possess anything; we are ourselves ineffably possessed. The individual hopes and fears, sorrows and desires that have so plagued our days are adjourned for the while. How can we, how dare we hold them when our own personal being is tightly held within an all-satisfying embrace?

During such unforgettable moments the Soul will speak plainly, if silently, to you. It may tell you about your true relationship to the universe and to your fellow creatures. It will certainly tell you about Itself. It may separate you from your body and let you gaze down upon it as from a height, long enough to permit you to comprehend that the flesh is quite the poorest and least significant part of you. And perhaps best of all it will certainly fill you with the assurance that after your return to the world of lonely struggle and quick forgetfulness, It will still remain beside and behind you.

* * *

Throughout the day, take advantage of odd moments to lift your mind to a higher level. The practice reveals positive qualities of strength and serenity not ordinarily known to be possessed.

* * *

If you accept the existence of a power behind the Universe which controls its life, which is perfect, and which is bringing all things and all beings—however slowly—closer to its own perfection, you must also accept the values of hope, improvement, and evolution while you must reject those of pessimism, deterioration, and nihilism. You will never feel sorry for yourself.

* * *

Intuition, inspiration, and even grace may come directly to you through prayer, meditation, and reading.

* * *

Meet your trials and temptations in the name and strength of your master, if you have one, or of the Overself, if you have not. Do not depend on the little ego alone.

* * *

If anyone or anything, a person or a book, can

contribute to free us from the resentments towards others or the bitternesses towards life which poison feelings, thoughts, and health, the person has rendered us a great service or the book has proved its worth.

✤ ✤ ✤

When a great crisis comes, always try to remember the spiritual teachings which the teacher has tried to impart to you, together with the indissoluble character of the inner tie that binds student and teacher together. Amidst all the dangers and hardships of the coming crisis, strive to keep open the inner channels of inspiration, protection, and guidance with the Divine Power. It will be very hard to do so under great outer pressures, but even two or three minutes of thought of it each day will be a help in this direction. The importance cannot be overestimated of simple recurring remembrance of (a) the Overself and (b) the teacher, and of trying to carry on in the atmosphere of such remembrance. It is a yoga path of its own and is as good in its way as any other. But if you cannot do more, even mere recollection for a minute of the mental image of the teacher will be a help.

✤ ✤ ✤

If in doubt regarding any great difficulty, close your eyes, think of a master, silently call on the master's name, then patiently wait. The force using him or her may come to your help.

■ ■ ■

The simple practice of holding the master's image in consciousness is enough to provide some protection in the world's temptations or dangers.

■ ■ ■

You may have lost your long-held fortune, your spouse may have shamefully betrayed you, your enemies may have spread false accusations against you, while your private world may have tumbled to pieces over your head. Still there remains something you have not lost, someone who has not betrayed you, someone who believes only the best about you, and an inner world that ever remains steady and unperturbed. That thing and that being are none other than your own Overself, which you may find within you, which you may turn to when in anguish, and which will strengthen you to disregard the clamant whine of the personal distress. If you do not do this, there is nothing else you can do. Whither can you turn save to the inner divinity?

■ ■ ■

Release your problems. Work in the Silence—until the Silence rules. The Infinite Intelligence will then take over your problems—to the extent that you release them to it.

■ ■ ■

When you feel the presence of a diviner self within

your breast, when you believe that its power protects and provides for you, when you view past errors and future troubles alike with perfect equanimity, you have a better capacity to enjoy life and a truer expression of happiness than those who delight only in ephemeral pleasures and sense satisfactions. For it will endure into times of adversity and last through hours of calamity, where the other will crumble and vanish.

✠ ✠ ✠

Unforgettable as the finding of secret wealth was the day when this Overself chose to make itself known to me. For I had reached a crisis in my life and could go no farther if this troubling of the air with harsh thoughts was not put right in the only way that it could be put right. Many are the adventures and manifold incidents that have befallen me since that time, both of woe and weal. But now they do not matter, nor do I deem them worth the trouble of recording. For the mists that lay about me began to die away, and I came to know that one does not walk alone. The Overself *is ever with you.* As the years unfolded the dark curtains of the future, a strange quiescence stole upon the heart when it placed its life upon the altar of obedience, and when it grew to accept each day as freely as the wandering nomad accepts the pitiless desert in which he was born. It then cast the shroud of care that enveloped it and turned from the tomb of unsatisfied desire. So I came to wrap myself round with the silken mantle of secret hidden Beauty and sought to let no bitter brooding, no storm of passion touch it.

❖ ❖ ❖

With filial joy I offer you this flower of days that whatever fragrance it may have shall tell of the days I spent at your side. My head was heavy and bowed with the sorry burden of earthly life; my feet had wandered long among the rocky places and then grew tired as a sleeping man, when your great love shone down upon it and warmed it into life until it took strong root in some soft earth. Is it not appropriate then that I cull the first blooms for your table? I count it one of the great things of my life that I am privileged to call you Friend. And I know if I know you at all, that I can do no greater deed in return than to speak to my fellows of the unforgettably beautiful stream into which you turned my little boat, broken and halting though the words of my stammering lips must needs be.

❖ ❖ ❖

To the degree that the intuitive element can displace all others for the rulership of your inner life, to that degree can a healing and guiding calm displace the emotion of moods and commotion of thought.

❖ ❖ ❖

Somewhere at the hidden core of your being there is light, goodness, power, and tranquillity.

❖ ❖ ❖

The practice of turning to the Overself for relief, help, guidance, or healing in a grievous crisis is most effective only when, first, the will acts resolutely to put away thoughts of anguish, second, the turn is made swiftly, and, third, the will continues to keep the mind dwelling steadily on the benefic qualities of its sacred object, idea, or declaration.

❖ ❖ ❖

Inspired sentences or phrases can be used as amulets against your own dark moods as stronger hands to hold on to during depressed moments or weak phases.

❖ ❖ ❖

The instant vigorous and continued practice of a declaration may change the state of mind in a few minutes from a negative one that is agitated or depressed to a positive one that is reposed or cheerful.

❖ ❖ ❖

There is another special value of the declaration, and that is found during the strains and struggles of living. If established previously by habit, it will be present and available, ready to use at any moment of need or crisis.

❖ ❖ ❖

The effectiveness of a Declaration depends also upon its being repeated with a whole mind and an undivided heart, with confidence in its power and sincere desire to rise up.

* * *

Declarations:

"In my real being I am strong, happy, and serene."

"Infinite Power, sustain me! Infinite Wisdom, enlighten me. Infinite Love, ennoble me."

"May I co-operate more and more with the Overself. May I do its will intelligently and obediently."

"I co-operate joyously with the higher purpose of my life."

"In my real self life is eternal, wisdom is infinite, beauty is imperishable, and power is inexhaustible. My form alone is human for my essence is divine."

"In every situation I keep calm and seek out the Intuitive that it may lead me."

"I look beyond the troubles of the moment into the eternal repose of the Overself."

"The Peace of God."

"I dwell in the Overself's calm."

* * *

What is newer than a new dawning day? What a chance it offers for the renewing of life too! And how better to do this than to take a positive affirmative

Declaration like, "I Am Infinite Peace!" as the first morning thought, and to hold it, and hold on to it, for those first few minutes which set the day's keynote? Then, whatever matters there will be to attend, or pressing weighty duties to be fulfilled, we shall carry our peace into the midst of them.

Learn to live by faith where you cannot live by sight, to accept happenings against which the ego rebels and to endure situations which reason denounces.

Our greatest strength comes from reliance on the Higher Self and faith in the Higher Laws.

This is the magic talisman which will strengthen and save you, even though you go down into Hades itself—this faith and love for the inner self.

Wherever the fortunes of life may take you and whatever the dangers it may bring you, I hope you will always keep the thought of the Divine Overself as the best talisman to cling to. It is in these terrible times that you may come to appreciate more than ever the value of faith in divine wisdom behind life and assured immortality after death.

When you feel that your life is in the hands of a higher power, your fortunes governed by great laws whose ultimate intent is utter beneficence, your courage will be unassailable.

Amid the confusions and dangers of today, this faith in a divine plan of the world can support us like a rock.

Under great strain and amid grave dangers, you will find courage and endurance in the talismanic power of remembering the Higher Self. It is always there.

You should dismiss fears and anxieties concerning the present state or future destiny of anyone you love. Do what you reasonably can to protect the other, then place him or her trustingly in the care and keeping of the higher power.

You will help others more by holding them mentally in this inner peace than by falling into a state of nervous anxiety about them.

Holding on to the future in anxiety and apprehension must be abandoned. It must be committed to the higher power completely and faithfully.

Calmness comes easily to one who really trusts the higher power. This is unarguable.

✤ ✤ ✤

Katherine Mansfield, the story writer, died early but not before she could write that the closing years of bodily suffering had changed her outlook on life. She had come from doubt about God to faith in God, from despair to a feeling that perfect Love behind the universe called for perfect trust from her. The tuberculous body, which had kept her so immobilized for so long a time, brought her nevertheless to a kind of meditation wherein she lay, feeling the stillness within grow more and more palpable and the aspiration to merge in it grow stronger and stronger.

✤ ✤ ✤

Even during the longest dark night of the soul, the Overself is not a whit less close to you than it was when it revealed its presence amid ecstasy and joy.

✤ ✤ ✤

One who has to bear a great trial in the course of conducting worldly business must, at such a time, look more than ever before to the higher power for sustenance and comfort. The more you are tried the greater the inner reward will be if you hold to the faith that is in you.

✤ ✤ ✤

Not to lose this inner peace amid difficulties which may crush others to the ground in despair, not to lose faith in this deeper source of fortitude and support—if this should be called for at a certain time in your life, you will only grow inwardly by taking the challenge, even if you fail outwardly by the seeming result.

✠ ✠ ✠

To put anxiety aside, which follows naturally when our personal attachment to results and the eager desire for ends are laid aside, is to have the fullest faith that the higher power will take care of our true needs.

✠ ✠ ✠

During times of war and suffering, the spiritual Quest demonstrates its value by the inner support which it gives and the unquenchable faith it bestows. The forces of evil will be checked; the good will triumph in the end, as always. God's love for all remains what it ever shall be—the best thing in life.

✠ ✠ ✠

Faith is needed to make the basic change in your thinking, the change which takes you out of the past's grip. A new life is possible if you take up new thoughts.

✠ ✠ ✠

As soon as we succumb to moods of despondency, hopelessness, and helplessness, we are doomed. As soon as we triumph over them, we are saved.

Life remains what it is—deathless and unbound. We shall all meet again. Know what you are, and be free. The best counsel today is, keep calm, *aware*. Don't let the pressure of mental environment break into what you know and what is real and ultimately true. This is your magic talisman to safeguard you; cling to it. The last word is—Patience! The night is darkest before dawn. But dawn comes.

Your mental attitude tells the story. It will take you up to heights supreme or it will cast you down into a sea of unutterable despair. Whatever you do, fight for the proper mental attitude.

Patience is the twin of hope.

The ability to hold on during a single dark period, when the frustrations and humiliations of poverty seem unbearable, may turn the fortunes of one's entire life for the better.

You seem, in this desolate "night," to be up against a blank wall. But with patience you may find a way out. It is well to remember Abraham Lincoln's "This too will pass."

If you fail but persist despite the failures, one day you will find yourself suddenly possessed of the power to win, the power to achieve what had hitherto seemed impossible for your limited ability. This gift—for it is nothing else—is Grace.

The aspirant who cries out in despair that he is unable either to make progress or to get a mystical experience and that Grace seems absent or indifferent does not understand that he has within himself, as every man has, a place which is the abode of Grace. When I say every man, I mean every human being—which includes the vast multitudes of non-aspirants too. Just as the exhausted athlete may with some patience find what he calls his second wind, so the man whose thought, feeling, will, and aspiration are exhausted may find his interior deeper resource; but this requires patience and passivity. The need to hope, to wait, and to be passive is the most important of all.

That which delays the expression of your dynamic

thought in modifications of your environment or alterations of your character is the weight of your own past karma. But it only delays; if you keep up the pressure of concentration and purpose, your efforts must eventually show their fruit.

■ ■ ■

Defeat is only an alarm clock calling you to get up and get going once more.

■ ■ ■

If outer events bring you to a position where you can bear them no longer and force you to cry out to the higher power in helplessness for relief, or if inner feelings bring humiliation and recognition of your dependence on that power, this crushing of the ego may open the door to grace.

■ ■ ■

To the degree that you can surrender your mind to the higher self, to that degree do you surrender the worries and fears that go along with it.

■ ■ ■

The passage from black despair to healing peace begins with learning to "let go." This can refer to the past's crippling pictures, the present's harsh conditions, or the future's grim anticipations. To what then can the sufferer turn? To the Overself and its divine power.

* * *

The same power which has brought you so far will surely carry you through the next phase of your life. You must trust it and abandon anxieties, as a passenger in a railroad train should abandon her bag by putting it down on the floor and letting the train carry it. The bag represents personal attempts to plan, arrange, and mold the future in a spirit of desire and attachment. This is like insisting on bearing the bag's weight oneself. The train represents the Higher Self to which you should surrender that future. Live in inner Peace, free from anticipations, desires, cares, and worries.

* * *

There are occasions when it is either prudent or wise to practise Stoic submission. But there are other occasions when it is needful to do battle with the event or the environment.

* * *

Trying in the wrong way hinders us and trying in the right way helps us. Rebellion against fate does not help; acceptance and correction of fate does.

* * *

Resignation to circumstance, adaptation to environment, coming to terms with the inevitable, and acceptance of the unavoidable, however reluctant —these have their place as much as the use of free aggressive will.

* * *

To strive hard for a worthwhile aim but to resign oneself to its abandonment if destiny is adverse to its realization, is not the same as to do nothing for it at all but to leave that aim entirely to fate. To eliminate within oneself the avoidable causes of misfortune and trouble but to endure understandingly those which are the unavoidable human lot is not the same as to let those causes remain untouched whilst blindly accepting their effects as fate.

* * *

When you have made this surrender, done what you could as a human being about it and turned the results over completely to the higher self, analysed its lessons repeatedly and taken them deeply to heart, the problem is no longer your own. You are set free from it, mentally released from its karma, whatever the situation may be physically. You know now that whatever happens will happen for the best.

* * *

Accept the long night patiently, quietly, humbly, and resignedly as intended for your true good. It is not a punishment for sin committed but an instrument of annihilating egoism.

* * *

It comes to this, that a man who is brought down by adverse events or by inward failure, who loses confidence in himself and hope for his future, who is stricken down by what John of the Cross called "the dark night of the soul" —such a man is unknowingly at a possible turning-point of his life. Let him surrender this poor crushed ego of his, this broken belief that he can successfully manage his life, and pray to the Overself to take it all over.

* * *

Let us have enough courage to face life yet let us not forget the need of enough humility to face our creator.

* * *

When you lose faith in your own goodness, and even your own capacities, to the point of despairing hopelessness, you are really ready to pray properly and practise utter dependence upon the Higher Power's grace. When you realize that the evil in yourself and in other people is so deep and so strong that there is nothing below the surface of things you can do, you are forced to turn to this Power. When you abandon further trust in your own nature and cling to no more personal hopes, you really let go of the ego. This gives you the possibility of being open to grace.

* * *

Anxieties subside and worries fall away when this surrender to the Overself grows and develops in your heart. And such a care-free attitude is not unjustified. For the measure of this surrender is also the measure of active interference in your affairs by the Divine Power.

✠ ✠ ✠

Whatever mental-emotional clouds the day may bring, do not detain them but let them pass over you. This would seem a superhuman feat, but it becomes possible when you turn them over to the higher power.

✠ ✠ ✠

Your troubles may at times leave you with a sense of frustration and defeat. This is natural. It simply means that a difficult hand is being dealt out to you by fate. You should appraise it philosophically as a general indication of the unsatisfactoriness of earthly life in the Buddhistic sense. On this path you get all kinds of vicissitudes and ups and downs, partly to demonstrate vividly that the inner reality is the only unchanging value and thus compel a resort to its quest, and partly to bring out latent qualities. But you will not be tried beyond what you can bear.

✠ ✠ ✠

When you can forgive God all the anguish of your past calamities and when you can forgive other men and women for the wrongs they have done you, you will come to inward peace. For this is what your ego cannot do.

✠ ✠ ✠

If you succeed in keeping out of the emotional surface of your being the temptation to take your situation rebelliously, and penetrate instead deep down inside where you can take it resignedly, you will gain strength and feel peace.

✠ ✠ ✠

The Inner Being will rise and reveal Himself just as soon as the ego becomes sufficiently humbled, subdued, surrendered. The assurance of this is certain because we live forever within the Love of God.

2

CULTIVATE REPOSE, SELF-RENEWAL

Grace is here for all. It cannot be here for one special person and not for another. Only we do not know how to open our tensioned hands and receive it, how to open our ego-tight hearts and let it gently enter.

There are situations which may seem beyond endurance and circumstances beyond sufferance. It is then that those who have learned how to withdraw into their interior being, how to return to their source, may find some measure of help and strength.

However dark or blundering the past, however miserable the tangle one has made of one's life, this unutterable peace blots it all out. Within that seraphic embrace error cannot be known, misery cannot be felt, sin cannot be remembered. A great cleansing comes over the heart and mind.

Outwardly one's life may suffer every kind of limitation, from bodily paralysis to miserable surroundings, but inwardly it is free in meditation to reach out to a sphere of light, beauty, truth, love, and power.

Most of one's misery is inflicted on oneself by accepting and holding negative thoughts. They cover and hide the still centre of one's being, which is infinite happiness.

We keep ourselves too occupied and then wonder why our nerves are taut, our minds without ease, our nights without sleep. One who knows the art of perfectly relaxing body, breath, and mind has a better chance to find health, poise, and peace.

❖ ❖ ❖

Try, so far as possible, to avoid anxiety about your problems, whether they are of a worldly or spiritual nature. It is necessary to develop a calm, hopeful attitude toward the future.

❖ ❖ ❖

At a certain depth of penetration into your inward being, pain of the body and misery of the emotions are unable to exist. They disappear from the meditator's consciousness.

❖ ❖ ❖

Amid the tumult of ego-directed thoughts and feelings, the distress brought on by an adverse circumstance which the ego has not been able to endure or set right can be lessened and relieved by relaxing, letting go, pausing, lying physically and mentally still, whether in a prayer for inner peace or a simple meditation, but in any case turning the affair over to the higher power as a sign of having let go. Such temporary withdrawal gives the Overself its chance to break through the ego's crust and to bring its ministering peace, help, guidance, or healing.

❖ ❖ ❖

Let go of the thoughts which make so much turmoil in the head, so much stress in the nerves, and enjoy the calm of Mental Quiet. This is more easily said than done. So bring in help—from the body, from profound sayings, from the exercises of both Long and Short Paths, and from the remembrance of God.

* * *

The worst troubles fall into better perspective when we enter into these withdrawn periods, when we look at them from the deeper self's poise.

* * *

When it seems humanly impossible to do more in a difficult situation, surrender yourself to the inner silence and thereafter wait for a sign of obvious guidance or for a renewal of inner strength.

* * *

If the concentrated attention can penetrate to a certain level of the mind in meditation, it will penetrate to a source of power and knowledge that is ordinarily hidden, unknown, neglected, or untapped. From this source one can draw guidance, engender strength, and obtain instruction.

* * *

Let us accept the invitation, ever-open, from the Stillness, taste its exquisite sweetness, and heed its silent instruction.

❖ ❖ ❖

Open yourself in these silent periods to new intuitive feeling, and if it directs you to any new course of action, it will give you the power needed for that course.

❖ ❖ ❖

From this deep calm, certain valuable qualities are born: courage when tragedy confronts you, strength when battles must be fought, and wise perception when problems arise.

❖ ❖ ❖

This is the refuge to which you must turn when troubled, this is the place of divine beatitude. Go into the silence; there you will find the strength to conquer.

❖ ❖ ❖

Whatever the trouble be which distresses you—be it physical or mental, personal or public, worldly or spiritual—there is one sure refuge to which you can always turn and return. If you have learned the art of being still, you can carry your trouble to the mind's outer threshold and leave it there, passing yourself into its innermost recess of utter serenity and carefree tranquillity. This is not a cowardly escapism or a foolish self-deception, although with the unphilosophical mystic it could be and often is. For when you emerge from the inner silence and pick up your trouble again, you will pick up also the strength to endure it bravely and the wisdom to deal with it rightly. This will always be the case if your approach is through philosophical mysticism, which makes inspired action and not inspired dreaming its goal. Furthermore, your contact with the inner Mind will set mysterious forces working on your behalf to solve the problem quite independently of your conscious effort and knowledge.

To enter this stillness is the best way to pray.

Your capacity to recover quickly from, and react positively to, the unexpected shocks of life will be one of the benefits of this cultivation of calmness.

Life, history, experience—each gives us the same clear message. The temple of Solomon, once a pyramid in its vast area, is felled to the ground, and its thousands of worshippers gone with it. What, then, how, and where shall we worship? Let us seek the timeless Power which transcends the centuries, let us utter no word but fall into silence, for here the voice of the little ego's thoughts is an insult. Let us go where Jesus advised—deep inside the heart. For we carry the truth within ourselves—yet how few know it—and bear the closest of ties with that Power in consciousness itself.

❖ ❖ ❖

It is a soothing experience to sit in the grass high on the top of a cliff, to look out at the vast spread of sea, and then to let the mind empty itself of accumulated problems. As the minutes pass, equanimity is restored and repose laps one about.

❖ ❖ ❖

When a sensitive person is in distress he or she will often, if circumstances allow, turn to nature, go to a wood, a forest, a meadow, a park, or even a small garden, either for a changed scene or to muse upon their situation. Why? It is an instinctive act. They need help, hope, comforting, guidance, or peace. The instinct is a true one, a response to a lead from one's higher self.

❖ ❖ ❖

You may go to the silent forest to take wordless comfort when in distress.

❖ ❖ ❖

When you are in deep trouble, for which no human voice can bring consolation, it is then the turn of Nature. In the quiet woods, the winding riverside, the view from a mountain, you may gather some crumbs, at least, of that which you cannot find elsewhere.

❖ ❖ ❖

The strong emotional impression of beauty which a Nature-painted scene can evoke will—if you stay with it and do not too quickly hurry off to other thoughts—take you away from self-consciousness, its narrow confines and severely limited interests. You forget them, and in the forgetting are released for the time from your ego.

* * *

The closer I come to Nature the farther I go from evil. I move towards her because I feel drawn by her beauty and healed by her peace, yet I find that virtue follows them not long after.

* * *

You may be gently influenced by such beauty of Nature to pause and gaze, holding yourself still for the while, admiring and appreciating the scene, until you are so absorbed that you are lost in it. The ego and its affairs retreat. Unwittingly you come close to the delicious peace of the Overself.

* * *

In the quiet woods or green meadows, or hearing the mountain streams bubbling along their downward way, your appreciation of Nature may rise to actual communion.

* * *

In the beauty which Nature can offer, you may find a catalyst to bring your feelings toward a loftier plane.

✠ ✠ ✠

There are moments when you may sit alone with nature, when no sound intrudes and all is quiet, pleasant, harmonious. If you will enter into this stillness with nature and enter it deeply enough, you will find that it is associated with what most religions call God.

✠ ✠ ✠

Why do the sensitive find the freedom of an open uninterrupted view across landscape or seascape so appealing? The largeness and freedom of space echo back from outside the body the same attributes of the Spirit within.

✠ ✠ ✠

Some magnificent play of sun on earth, ocean, or sky may provide a spectacle to hold sense and mind alike enthralled. The effect on feeling may deepen to the point where a sense of uplift, exaltation, and peace becomes overwhelming. This is rare, memorable vision, where faith in an intelligent Power behind things is restored or fortified. It will pass completely, it may even never recur again, but it cannot be forgotten.

✠ ✠ ✠

What could be more important symbolically or more pleasing aesthetically than to watch the shining sun rise from behind mountains or over seas? What hope it gives, what help it promises to all beings and not only to humankind. What too could be more beautiful and more tranquillizing than to watch the same sun setting in the evening?

❖ ❖ ❖

The evening sunfall brings its own beauty, declaims its own poetry. It is worth the waiting in the short period before Nature's holy pause, when one can share her peace with one's soul, her mystery with one's mind, and feel her kinship with one's self. As the dusk deepens there is a shift of standpoint and basic truths come into sight or become more clear. The heart and its feelings are affected, too—purified, ennobled, enriched.

❖ ❖ ❖

However hard-pressed, troubled, or fatigued your day has been, this is the hour which relieves—even saves—it, this pause harmonized with Nature's own pause.

❖ ❖ ❖

It is as if the sun gave a last lingering kiss to this earth, a farewell greeting to act as a reminder to hold on to hope.

❖ ❖ ❖

How valuable are those moments when one finds time "to stand and stare" at some bit of Nature's floral beauty or arboreal colour, or to listen in the right way to music. Much beauty that you did not notice before will now be discovered and severe tensions will vanish.

Music can express the mystical experience better than language; it can tell of its mystery, joy, sadness, and peace far better than words can utter. The fatigued intellect finds a tonic and the harassed emotions find comfort in music.

To recognize, appreciate, or create beauty is to bring gladness into life.

In the admiration of Nature's beauty and the appreciation of art, music, poetry, and literature, you can find sources of inner help and themes for meditation.

What, it has been asked, if I get no glimpses? What can I do to break this barren, monotonous, dreary, and sterile spiritual desert of my existence? The answer is if you cannot meditate successfully go to nature, where she is quiet or beautiful; go to art where it is majestic, exalting; go to hear some great soul speak, whether in private talk or public address; go to literature, find a great inspired book written by someone who has had the glimpses.

❖ ❖ ❖

3

TROUBLES AS TEACHERS

In one sense troubles are our teachers and the greater the trouble the greater the teaching impressioned upon us.

If what you are undergoing is hard to endure, it is also an opportunity that will not recur again in the same form and under the same circumstances, an opportunity to master a special lesson or to arouse a latent energy or to work on a particular character-trait.

Even trouble can be turned to self-educative uses, and some kind of benefit gained out of the experience. But this can happen more easily and more quickly only if the willingness to learn is there, and only if a corresponding surrender of self is present. It is then that so-called evil is converted to so-called good.

Now and then karma unloads trials and troubles which are not pleasant to endure. All the same they have something to teach us—if only the ancient lesson of the need to find a more satisfactory inner life to compensate for the transiency and the vicissitudes of the outer life. You cannot escape from these so long as you live upon this earth but you can hope to understand them and eventually to master your mental reactions to them. Therein lies peace and wisdom.

Most persons have no inclination to wake up when dreams are pleasant, whereas when they are frightening they soon awaken. So too the dream of worldly life does not impress them with the need of true religion until it becomes tragic or severely disappointing. Only when sorrow drives them to question the value of living do they take a real interest in nonworldly urges.

✦ ✦ ✦

Human nature is universally frail; yours is no exception. Nevertheless, if you are appalled at your mistakes, if this anguish is doubled because what you have done wrongly is irreparable, is there nothing else left to do than to give yourself up to helpless despair? The true answer is more hopeful than that. "I know that if I keep patient while cultivating humility and silencing the ego's pride, I shall grow away from old weaknesses and overcome former mistakes"—this should be the first stage of your new attitude. For the next one, you can at least go over the events of the past and amend them in thought. You can put right mentally those wrong decisions and correct those rash impulsive actions. You can collect the profits of lessons expensively learnt.

✦ ✦ ✦

It is through meeting and understanding the difficulties on the path, through facing and mastering them, that we grow. Each of us in this world lives in a state of continuous struggle, whatever outward appearances to the contrary may suggest. Repose is for the dead alone—and then only for a limited time. We must study the lessons behind every experience, painful or pleasant, that karma brings. We lose nothing except what is well worth losing if we frankly acknowledge past errors. Only vanity or selfishness can stand in the way of such acknowledgement. Earthly life is after all a transient means to an enduring end. The worth or worthlessness of its experiences lies not in any particular external form, but in the development of consciousness and character to which they lead. Only after time has cooled down the fires of passion and cleared the mists of self-interest are most people able to perceive that these mental developments are the essential and residual significance of their human fortunes. With the seeker after truth, the period of meditation must be devoted, at least in part, to arriving at such perceptions even in the midst of life's events.

The place where you are, the people who surround you, the problems you encounter, and the happenings that take place just now—all have their special meaning for you. They come about under the law of recompense as well as under the particular needs of your spiritual growth. Study them well but impersonally, egolessly, and adjust your reactions accordingly. This will be hard and perhaps even unpalatable, yet it is the certain way to solving all your problems. This is what Jesus meant when he declared, "If any man will come after me, let him deny himself, and take up his cross daily, and follow me." This is that crucifixion of the ego which is true Christianity and which leads directly to the resurrection in the reality of the Overself. Regard your worst, most irritating trouble as the voice of your Overself. Try to hear what It says. Try to remove the obstructions It is pointing to within yourself. Look on this special ordeal, this particular trial, as having the most important significance in your own spiritual growth. The more crushing it is, the more effort is being made to draw you nearer to the Overself. At every point of your life, from one event, situation, contact to another, the Infinite Intelligence provides you with the means of growth, if only you will get out of the egoistic rut and take them.

✠ ✠ ✠

It is true that every happening in the outer life can be accepted as being good for the inner life, that the most calamitous situation can be taken as God's will for us. But it is also true that unless we ask—and correctly answer—in what sense it is good and why it is God's will, we may fail to seek out and strive to correct the fault in us which makes it good and providential. For each situation presents not only the need and opportunity of recognizing a higher power at work in our life, but also a problem in self-examination and self-improvement.

✠ ✠ ✠

Do not give way to feelings of despair about the long

road ahead of you. You may go far in this incarnation, particularly after you begin to recognize your "failures" for the stepping-stones they are, and to use the knowledge and discrimination gained from these experiences to safeguard your future progress from similar mishaps. Besides, you are not alone in your efforts and help *is* available.

Because the Mind at the back of the Universe's life is infinitely wise, there is always a reason for what happens to us. It is better therefore not to rail at adverse events but to try to find out why they are there. It may be consoling to blame others for them, but it will not be helpful. If we look within ourselves for the causes, we take the first step toward bringing adversity to an end; if we look outside, we may unnecessarily prolong it.

Life will bring you, if you are teachable, through the tutelage of bitter griefs and ardent raptures to learn the value of serenity. But if you are not, then the great oscillations of experience will tantalize you until the end.

The kind of experience which you most dislike to have is the very kind which forces you to seek out its cause, and thus begin unwittingly the search for life's meaning. The disappointments in your emotional life, the sufferings in your physical body, and the misfortunes in your personal fate ought to teach you to discriminate more carefully, to examine more deeply, and in the end to feel more sympathy with the sorrowing.

❖ ❖ ❖

Indeed, the hour may come when, purified from the ego's partiality, you will kiss the cross that brought you such agony and when, healed of your blindness, you will see that it was a gift from loving hands, not a curse from evil lips. You will see too that in your former insistence on clinging to a lower standpoint, there was no other way of arousing you to the need and value of a higher one than the way of unloosed suffering. But at last the wound has healed perfectly leaving you, as a scar of remembrance, greatly increased wisdom.

❖ ❖ ❖

Awakening to the need of the Divine may come through some mental crisis or emotional shock which shakes the whole of your being to its deepest foundations. It is out of the suffering and grief produced by such a situation that you plant the first trembling steps on the secret path. It is such outer torments of life that shatter inner resistance so that the need for spiritual help is acknowledged. And the more unsatisfactory outward life becomes, the more satisfactory does the blessed inward life seem both by contrast and in itself.

* * *

Out of suffering may come the transmutation of values, even the transfiguration of character. But these developments are possible only if you cooperate. If you do not, then the suffering is in vain, fruitless.

* * *

The great error of all these worldly-happiness Spiritual teachings like New Thought, Unity, Christian Science, and especially Dr. Peale's "Power of Positive Thinking" is that they have no place for pain, sorrow, adversity, and misfortune in their idea of God's world. They are utterly ignorant of the tremendous truth, voiced by *every* great prophet, that by divine decree the human lot mixes good and bad fortune, health, events, situations, and conditions; that suffering has been incorporated into the scheme of things to prevent humanity from becoming fully satisfied with a sensual existence. They demand only the pleasant side of experience. If this demand were granted, they would be deprived of the chance to learn all those valuable and necessary lessons which the unpleasant side affords and thus deprived of the chance ever to attain a full knowledge of spiritual truth. It is the ego which is the real source of such a limited teaching. Its desire to indulge itself rather than surrender itself is at the bottom of the appeal which these cults have for their unwary followers. These cults keep aspirants tied captive within the personal ego, limit them to its desires. Of course, the ego in this case is disguised under a mask of spirituality.

✤ ✤ ✤

If you overdo your remorse and stretch out your repentance too far; if your self-examination and self-criticism become unreasonably prolonged and unbearably overconcentrated, the actuating motive will then be not true humility but neurotic pity for yourself.

✤ ✤ ✤

Listen to the message experience is trying to give you, then learn it and obey it.

✤ ✤ ✤

When every situation which life can offer is turned to the profit of spiritual growth, no situation can really be a bad one.

✤ ✤ ✤

All worldly experiences may become doors to divinity if interpreted aright.

✤ ✤ ✤

The experiences which come to you and the circumstances in which you find yourself are not meaningless. They usually have a personal karmic lesson for you and should be studied much more than books. You must try to understand impersonally the inner significance behind these events. Their meaning can be ascertained by trying to see them impartially, by evaluating the forces which are involved in them, by profound reflection, and by prayer. Each person gets his or her special set of experiences, which no one else gets. Each life is individual and gets from the law of recompense those which it really needs, not those which someone else needs. The way in which you react to the varied pleasant and unpleasant situations which develop in everyday life will be a better index to the understanding you have gained than any mystical visions painted by the imagination.

Neither suffering alone nor joy alone can educate your heart and develop your mind in the right way. Both are needed.

The lessons of past experience are not enough in themselves to provide all the guidance needed for present living. We need also the ideals held up by intuition, the principles and ideas presented from within by the higher part of our nature, and from without by the spiritual teachers and religious prophets of humankind.

It would be easy to misconceive the philosophic attitude towards these negative feelings: anxiety, worry, fear, indignation, and righteous wrath. Philosophy does not teach us to avoid facing the situation or circumstance which gave rise to any of these feelings, but only to avoid the negative reaction to it. It tells us to learn all we can from it, to understand why it is there at all, to analyse its meaning and apply its lesson. Only after this has been done, and especially only after we have attended to the correction of whatever fault or failing in us helped to create the situation, are we advised to forget it, turn our face away, and calmly put ourselves to rest in thoughts and remembrances of the impersonal Overself. Only then is our sorrow and suffering to be discarded, and we are to recall that there is no room for despair in the truth. That reflective wisdom must be followed by courage and even joy.

✽ ✽ ✽

Wisdom is needed to make the most of life. The discipline of character is needed to prevent avoidable suffering. The control of thought is needed to attain peace. Reverence for the highest is needed for spiritual fulfilment.

✽ ✽ ✽

Self-control is your greatest friend through all the incidents and accidents of life.

✽ ✽ ✽

They are competent to deal with life who equip themselves to deal with its darker sides as well as with its brighter ones, with its difficulties and sufferings no less than with its joys and successes.

✤ ✤ ✤

Our deliverance from the miseries of life hangs solely on our deliverance from the bondage to the ego.

✤ ✤ ✤

The worst misfortune is not to experience it but to misunderstand it, and consequently misinterpret it. When it makes us worse in character than before, less in faith than before, when it fills us with resentment bitterness anger or hatred, it is *we* who are injured and not merely our fortunes.

✤ ✤ ✤

The psychological laws governing the inner development of spiritual seekers often seem to operate in most mysterious ways. The very power whose presence you may think has been denied you—Grace—is taking care of you even when you are not conscious of this fact. The more the anguish, at such a time, the more the Higher Self is squeezing the ego. The more you seem to be alone and forsaken, the closer the Higher Self may be drawing you to Itself.

✤ ✤ ✤

If you could assume a perfectly impersonal point of view you would be able to see how much of your spiritual development you owe to heartache, loss, and suffering which you once complained about or regarded pessimistically. You would then understand how these very factors have helped immeasurably to deepen your determination, sharpen your intelligence, and, above all, improve your character.

* * *

On one thing all people in all lands are agreed, that it is immeasurably more preferable to be released from anxieties than to suffer them. Yet, these same people throw themselves into situations or bring about events which will rivet the chains of anxiety upon them. How is it that such a contradiction exists everywhere? What causes them to do this? It is the strength of their desires, the power of their ambitions, the tendencies inherited from past births. This being the cause of the trouble, the remedy for it becomes plain. The more you free yourself from desires, that is, the more you master yourself, the more are you freed from numerous anxieties. And even if you too are subject to the painful tests and unpleasant ordeals which inescapably affect human existences, you do not consider them to be misfortunes but as devices to draw out your latent qualities.

* * *

No one may free oneself from every form of outward suffering but all may free themselves from inward suffering.

* * *

Each difficulty surmounted, each weakness resisted will fortify your will and increase your perseverance.

It will evoke the better part of your nature and discipline the baser, and thus fit you more adequately to cope with the next ones.

✠ ✠ ✠

Every time you take the harder way of acknowledging a fault, repenting a wrong, and then earnestly seeking to make reparation to whoever has suffered by it, you will be repaid by the sudden descent of gratifying peace, of a happy serenity absent from ordinary hours.

✠ ✠ ✠

To eradicate anger you should cultivate its opposite —forgiveness.

✠ ✠ ✠

Ordinarily it is not easy, not natural, to forgive anyone who has wronged us. The capacity to do so will come to us as understanding grows large enough or as meditation penetrates deep enough or as grace blesses us.

✠ ✠ ✠

The moral purification involved in casting out all hatred and granting complete forgiveness opens a door to the Overself's light.

✠ ✠ ✠

All experience shows what distress and misery often follow undisciplined passion and unruled feeling.

✽ ✽ ✽

Outward changes for the better are almost always the result of improved inner conditions—that is, better, more inspired thinking, plus elimination of negative thoughts and actions.

✽ ✽ ✽

When we are brought face-to-face with the consequences of our wrong-doing, we would like to avoid the suffering or at least to diminish it. It is impossible to say with any precision how far this can be done for it depends partly on Grace, but it also depends partly on ourselves. We can help to modify and sometimes even to eliminate those bad consequences if we set going certain counteracting influences. First, we must take to heart deeply the lessons of our wrong-doing. We should blame no one and nothing outside of ourselves, our own moral weaknesses and our own mental infirmities, and we should give ourselves no chance for self-deception. We should feel all the pangs of remorse and constant thoughts of repentance. Second, we must forgive others their sins against us if we would be forgiven ourselves. That is to say, we must have no bad feelings against anyone whatsoever or whomsoever. Third, we must think constantly and act accordingly along the line which points in an opposite direction to our wrong-doing. Fourth, we must pledge ourselves by a sacred vow to try never again to commit such wrong-doing. If we really mean that pledge, we will often bring it before the mind and memory and thus renew it and keep it fresh and alive. Both the thinking in the previous point and the pledging in this point must be as intense as possible. Fifth, if need be and if we wish to do so, we may pray to the Overself for the help of its Grace and pardon in this matter; but we should not resort to such prayer as a matter of course. It should be done only at the instigation of a profound inner prompting and under the pressure of a hard outer situation.

If untoward circumstances obscure our pleasure in life and obstruct our aims in life, they also teach us something of the ultimate truth about life. If we react to them according to the blind instincts of the ego, they plunge us into greater darkness: if, however, we react according to the inner promptings of the Overself, they lead us toward greater light.

If philosophy cannot show a way out of any particular distress, it can show how to refresh the heart's endurance of it and renew the mind's facing towards it.

Your own attitude towards events holds the power to make them good or bad, whatever their nature of itself may be.

If circumstances cannot be changed, they may be modified. If they cannot be modified, they may be viewed with a changed attitude of mind.

✠ ✠ ✠

The great ills (miscalled evils) of bodily life, such as disease and poverty, are often forced upon us by an implacable fate. But it would be a delusion to class them always with the great evils of mental life, such as hate and cruelty. For their control is frequently beyond our power, and their course may have to be endured, whereas sinful thoughts and their resultant deeds are not independent of our control and may be avoided.

✠ ✠ ✠

When you hit upon tragic times and difficult circumstances, the essential thing is to try within your power, however humbly that may be, to *live* the spiritual Quest. This is harder to do than ever before, yet it is almost more necessary than ever before. You must keep up your endeavours to understand and to practise what is right. Although great patience is called for during such times, great benefits will also show themselves in the end.

✠ ✠ ✠

The coming of war brings its own anxieties. This is when you have to draw upon your spiritual knowledge to get the strength and courage to endure bravely special trials and tribulations. It is only at such times of crisis that all higher interests get the chance to prove their solid worth, for without their inner support and some kind of understanding of what it all means, life becomes most inhumanly alarming. You may have found glimpses of inner peace from time to time and now you have to insert these into your external life and try to stretch them out through constant remembrance of the Real. Such frequent communion and intelligent remembrance can give you the strength to go on, the peace to put up with frustrations, doubts, and fears, and faith in what is still beyond your conscious knowledge, the satisfaction that the years are not being wasted. All other duties become better fulfilled when you fulfil this supreme duty of realizing the ever-present reality within the heart. Indeed they cannot be separated from it for through them Reality can express itself.

✠ ✠ ✠

As I sit at this oaken table and face my future, I can now do so without worry and with an almost complete calm. I realize now what I have but dimly realized before, that though the agonies which will yet come to me will be no less real than the agonies which have gone before, there remains a vast freedom of action to mold the man within me who has to *endure* those agonies. I know now that I can build up the figure and form of a great hero within the small space of my heart; that this hero can fight the darkest fate with bravery and with determination; but that if defeat is starred to come, he will smile and say, "This, too, will pass," and not be too bitter about it. I *can mold* this inner man; and I *will* do so.

This, then, is my future; the fortunes or misfortunes of fate are the lesser part; the soul that meets and fights that fate is the greater part; and that soul can be shaped by *my own* hands.

* * *

You must climb out of the dark pit of emotional resentment and self-pity into which the blows of life throw you. You should extirpate all the human and pardonable weakness which made you unhappy. You should be big-hearted and generous towards the failings of others who, you feel, have wronged you. It is a grand chance to make a quick spurt in your spiritual progress if you could change from the conventional emotional reaction to the philosophic and calmer one, if you could rise at one bound above what Rupert Brooke called "the long littleness of life." You should not continue to bear resentment against those who have wronged you, nor to brood over what they have done; forget the mean, the sordid, and the wicked things other people do and remember the great, the noble, and the virtuous things that you seek to do. Follow Jesus' example and cheerfully forgive, even unto seventy times seven. By your act of forgiveness to them, you will be forgiven yourself for the wrongs you also have done.

In their pardon lies your own. This is the law. In this way you demonstrate that you are able to leap swiftly from the present self-centered standpoint to a higher one, and you deal the personal ego a single paralysing blow. This is without doubt one of the hardest efforts anybody can be called upon to make. But the consequences will heal the wounds of memory and mitigate the pains of adversity.

When you are up against an especially difficult situation for which no immediate solution can be found, it will help you if you will use the time while waiting for the change—which will come—in order to deliberately cultivate greater patience and forebearance, as well as a more objective attitude.

There is no situation so bad, no predicament so undesirable, no crisis so formidable that it cannot be transformed, either in its physical actuality or in our mental picture of it, into a good. But this requires a willingness to work upon it spiritually, that is, egolessly.

You should begin by searching through your feelings to discover which one, if it exists, is the block to a speedier and favourable end to the trouble, which one is shutting out the forces of help, as well as which one is blinding you to the vital lesson behind the situation.

❖ ❖ ❖

It is during the periods of test that you must hold on to balance more than at other times.

❖ ❖ ❖

Those who turn cruel destiny or harsh accident to opportunity by taking a spiritual profit from it, abandoning natural bitterness and emotional rebellion, coming creatively in mind and positively in feeling to their suffering, thereby bring about its redemption.

❖ ❖ ❖

You may react to the experiences of life and the course of events with either the animal part of your nature or the spiritual part. The choice is yours.

❖ ❖ ❖

When confronted by a formidable situation involving human weakness or expressing human evil, affirm silently some great eternal truth covering the situation rather than letting yourself be discouraged by it.

❖ ❖ ❖

Every test is a teacher to guide us to a higher level, a providential friend to give us the quality we most need.

A difficult or frightening situation must be considered a challenge. At such a time, seek even more intensely through prayer, meditation, and faith—while also practising self-control to the best degree you are able — to achieve the needed spiritual strength and understanding in order to endure and overcome your troubles. In times of actual danger, the calm remembrance of the Overself will help to protect you.

Your moral response to a happening, as also your mental attitude toward it and emotional bearing under it, are largely free. It is in this realm, moreover, that important possibilities of further spiritual growth or else materialistic hardening are available. You may renew inner strength or fall back into sensual weakness.

The iron of human character turns to tempered steel in the white-hot furnace of trouble.

In the individual life it mostly happens that grace descends only after a period of great suffering. In humanity's life it is the same. Only when war and crises have run their course will new spiritual light be shed on us.

✥ ✥ ✥

The education of human intelligence, the culture of spiritual intuition, and the ennoblement of character are necessities, since it is they, together, that stand between humankind and catastrophe.

✥ ✥ ✥

Those who have much faith in the benevolent intentions of the Mind behind the universe, sooner or later find that faith severely tested. For the calamities of human life come to all of us.

✥ ✥ ✥

Those who take to this spiritual road have to endure its tests. It is not enough to have faith or feel spiritual when life's course is smooth and fortunate. They must learn to hold their faith and feeling when its course runs through difficulties and sickness also. If the test reveals that they lose their hold at such times, then it shows their need of doing further work on themselves. For this failure shows that they want good fortune and good health even more than they want to fulfil the higher spiritual purpose of their incarnation.

✥ ✥ ✥

Every test successfully met is rewarded by some growth in intuitive knowledge, strengthening of character, or initiation into a higher consciousness.

✥ ✥ ✥

Out of this ego-crushing, pride-humbling experience you may rise, chastened, heedful, and obeisant to the higher will.

* * *

Make up your mind that your attitude towards every experience counts more than the experience itself, that the way you think of it will either help or hurt your spiritual evolution. If your reaction to an event weakens your character and dulls your intuition, then it is really an evil one for you; if, however, your reaction is to utilize it for your spiritual growth, then it will in the end be a fortunate event.

* * *

In the giant mills where steel is prepared, we may glean a great lesson. The crude material is first made to undergo the ordeal of fire, a fire so intense that the material loses its solidity and becomes a bubbling liquid. And after its temperature has been lowered sufficiently to resume a solid form again, the still red-hot material has to undergo a further ordeal. It is hammered on every side, pounded from top to bottom. Out of these processes there emerges at last a purified, strengthened, finely tempered steel which will stand up to the most trying tests during wear and work. Men and women who wish to make something of their lives must take the terrific pounding and suffering to which they have had to submit as a similar process intended to turn away the dross in their character and strengthen the nobility within it.

✱ ✱ ✱

The test will come with every major crisis, every minor ordeal. If your inner work has been well done you will be surprised at the calmness with which you meet and pass the event, astonished at your strength.

✱ ✱ ✱

Another cause of illness is that God sends us tests and ordeals on this path, which may take the form of illness. But in that case we emerge spiritually stronger and wiser, if they are passed, and so benefit.

✱ ✱ ✱

It is the unexpected situation, when there is no time to calculate a response or prepare a reply, that reveals what measure of strength we can rise to. It is in the sudden crisis—which is only a situation pushed to a complete extreme—when there is no chance to escape altogether or to evade partially, that what wisdom we have, or lack, shows itself.

✱ ✱ ✱

One who can rise superior to circumstances, crises, or vicissitudes is an admirable character, but we deem such a person hardly human. Thus we have hypnotized ourselves into a negative complex. But the really great ones are not superhuman, they are truly human. It is for us to be what we divinely are; this the sages have perceived and accomplished.

* * *

When the ego is brought to its knees in the dust, humiliated in its own eyes, however esteemed or feared, envied or respected in other people's eyes, the way is opened for Grace's influx. Be assured that this complete humbling of the inner person will happen again and again until you are purified of all pride.

* * *

Only when your ego's pride has been shattered, only when you have become depressed by future prospects and humiliated by present failure, are you more likely to listen to the truth about yourself.

4

HEALING

The first principle of healing is to stop the obstructive resistance of the little ego so carried away by the belief that it can successfully manage its own life. The method of doing this is to cast out all negative thoughts, all destructive feelings, and all excessive egoisms. The second principle is to attune the individual to the universal life-force. The method of doing this is to learn the art of relaxing body and mind.

The healing powers of Nature truly exist, quite apart from the medical powers evoked by physicians, but they exist like electricity. To benefit by them we must draw them, focus them, and concentrate them on ourselves. This is done by our strong and sufficient faith, by our own concentration of attention, and by our relaxing and stilling of the whole being.

* * *

Healing Exercise and Meditation: (1) Lie flat on back on flat surface (for example, rug on floor). (2) Let body go completely limp. (3) Relax breathing with eyes shut, that is, slow down breathing below normal. Slowly exhale, then inhale; hold breath two seconds, then exhale slowly again. Repeat for three to five minutes. While inhaling, think that you are drawing in curative force from Nature. While exhaling, think that there is being taken out of your body the ill condition. (Note that on the inhaled breath, you—the ego—are referred to as the active agent, whereas in the exhaled breath this is not so and the change is being effected spontaneously.) (4) Let go all personal problems. (5) Reflect on the existence of the soul which is you, and on the infinite life-power surrounding you and in which you dwell and live. (6) Lie with arms outstretched and palms open, so as to draw in life-force either through palms or through head. (This makes contact with higher power through silent meditation, and it draws on the reconstructive and healing life-force attribute of this power.) Draw it into yourself. Let it distribute itself over the entire body. Let its omnintelligence direct it to where it is most needed, whether that be the affected part or some other part that is the first cause of the sickness. (7) Place hands on affected part of body and deliberately direct force through hands to body. A feeling of warmth should be noticeable in palms of hands. (8) Recollect through imagination the all-pervading sense of God and his infinite goodness.

✠ ✠ ✠

Healing Exercise: Inhale deeply but slowly and unhurriedly. With each breath fix the mind in the life-essence pouring in and permeating each part of the body until the whole of it is bathed and held by the stream.

✠ ✠ ✠

It is possible to direct the healing power of the white light, in imagination and with deep breathing, to any part of the body where pain is felt or to any organ which is not functioning properly. This does not instantly remove the trouble, but it does make a contribution towards the healing process.

✠ ✠ ✠

What happens during these relaxed moods? The focus of the conscious mind is withdrawn from the flesh and the vital centres, leaving the unconscious mind in sole sovereignty over them. What results from this? The destruction of the body's tissue is repaired, the fatigue of its nervous and muscular systems is removed. The fuller the relaxation, and the soul activity within, the fuller the recuperation.

✠ ✠ ✠

The attunement of your mind to the Universal Mind, of your heart to the fundamental love behind things, is capable of producing various effects. One of them may be the healing of bodily ills.

✠ ✠ ✠

We know that people can worry themselves into a state of physical sickness, but there seems to be less acceptance for the opposite idea that emotions and thoughts can also produce healing and not injury.

✠ ✠ ✠

"I had a joyous certainty that deafness and blindness were not an essential part of my existence since they were not in any way a part of my immortal mind."
—Helen Keller in *Midstream,* her autobiography

✠ ✠ ✠

If the pain is there, racking the physical life, the peace exists behind it, permeating the inner life.

✠ ✠ ✠

The assertion that Jesus primarily wished to free

people of disease, or to teach them how to become so, is untenable. Whoever has entered into the consciousness of his or her divine soul—which Jesus had in such fullness—has their whole scale of values turned over. It is then that they see that the physical is ephemeral by nature, whereas the reality whence it is derived is eternal by nature; that what happens inside one's heart and head is fundamentally more important than what happens inside one's body; and that the divine consciousness may and can be enjoyed even though the fleshly tenement is sick.

✚ ✚ ✚

Sufferers should use whatever physical medical means are available—both orthodox and unorthodox ones. At the same time they should practise daily prayer. But they should not directly ask for the physical healing for its own sake. They should ask first for spiritual qualities and then only for the physical healing with the expressed intention of utilizing the opportunity of bodily incarnation to improve themselves spiritually.

✚ ✚ ✚

The art of healing needs all the contributions it can get, from all the worthy sources it can find. It cannot realize all its potentialities unless it accepts them all: the homeopath along with the allopath, the naturopath along with the chiropractor, the psychiatrist along with the spiritual ministrant. It does not need them all together at one and the same time, of course, but only as parts of its total resources. A philosophic attitude refuses to bind itself exclusively to any single form of cure.

✠ ✠ ✠

A wise system of healing would coordinate physical and psychological, artificial and natural, dietary and spiritual treatments, using some or all of them as a means to the end—cure. But as the spiritual is the supreme therapeutic agent—if it can be touched—it will always be the one last resort for the desperate and chronic sufferers when all other agents have had to accept defeat.

✠ ✠ ✠

Dismayed by the failure of my physicians' last resort, I was sitting up in bed reading a passage from an old journal of John Wesley about spiritual healing. It quoted a friend as saying: "I could not move from place to place, but on crutches. In this state I continued about six years. At Bath I sent for a physician but before he came, as I sat reading the Bible, I thought, 'Asa sought to the physicians, and not to God; but God can do more for me than any physician'; soon after rising up, I found I could stand. From that time I have been perfectly well."

As soon as I finished this passage I thought it should be applied to my own case, and laid the book aside. A great mental stillness and inner indrawing came over me at the same time. I saw that all the methods hitherto used to eliminate the disease were futile precisely because they were the ego's own methods, whether physical, magical, mental, or mechanical. I had exhausted them all. So the ego had to confess its total failure and cast itself on the mercy of the higher power in humiliation and prayer. I realized that instead of thinking that *I* or my physicians were competent to cure the disease, the correct way was to disbelieve that and to look to the Overself alone for healing. I saw that the stillness was its grace, that this quietness was its power. It could best cure me, if only I would relax and let it enter. So I surrendered to it and within a few weeks was healed.

✠ ✠ ✠

It is impossible either to guarantee or to predict what would happen in any individual case. The difficulty is that if you try to get at the Truth simply as a means to achieve the healing, the Truth eludes you. You have therefore to seek Truth and leave your fate to it, which will always work out for the best, materially or otherwise.

✠ ✠ ✠

If you want to heal someone do not concentrate upon the nature of their disease, or you may strengthen it. Concentrate rather upon the nature of their Overself, that its mighty grace may be released to them. Do not even pray that he or she will be cured. Pray rather that the power of the Overself's grace may work within them, and do what it will.

* * *

We eagerly seek to be relieved of sickness or trouble, but where relief is followed by a feeling of relationship to the Overself, we have gained something far more valuable than we originally sought.

* * *

The pains and maladies which accompany and punctuate physical existence are not taken away from a person who is spiritually aware. Their presence continues to act as a reminder—as much to him or her as to all other people—that just because they do accompany the body's life, that life is an imperfect and unsatisfying one. Their five senses are working like all other people's and so must report the painful as well as pleasurable sensations. But what such a person does gain is a peace deeper than the body's sensations, and unbreakable by their painful nature. One part of them—the lesser—may suffer; but the other part—the greater—remains undisturbed. In their higher and spiritual nature they are well fortified against these afflictions, sustained by heavenly forces denied to other people.

* * *

The Overself does have the power to heal the diseases

of the body by its Grace, but whether that Grace will be thus exercised or not is unpredictable. It will do what is best for the individual in the ultimate sense, not what the ego desires. For the Divine Wisdom is back of everything every time.

■ ■ ■

The treatment of unpleasant realities by not including them in one's picture of the world comforts but at the same time befools a person. None of the great prophets like Jesus and Buddha denied the existence of sickness, the reality of pain, or the significance of suffering in the cosmos. No—they acknowledged them as being inseparable from human life but pitied the victims and offered them an inward comfort which was based on truth and reality.

■ ■ ■

That Power which brought the body into existence originally maintains its involuntary functions, cures its diseases, and heals its wounds. It is within the body itself; it is the life-force aspect of the Soul, the Overself. Its curative virtue may express itself through various mediums—as herbs and foods, hot, cold, or mud baths, and deep breathings, exercise, and osteopathy—or it may express itself by their complete absence as in fasting, often the quickest and most effective medium. Or, disdaining physical methods entirely, it may act directly and almost miraculously as spiritual healing.

❖ ❖ ❖

Nature is an expression of the Universal Mind. The plants are given to us for medicine or food. It is an insult to Nature to despise these remedies.

❖ ❖ ❖

Nature not only soothes troubled minds but heals troubled bodies. She provides them with curative herbs, barks, waters, rays, leaves—the woods are sanitariums.

❖ ❖ ❖

A monk who attained great renown and reputation in Rumania for his selfless character, inspired preaching, and miraculous healing said that he asked all patients to make a confession privately to him of their wrong attitudes and wrong-doing before the work of healing could begin, as this opened the door.

❖ ❖ ❖

Continued ill health is a great trial. The very fact that an individual has been forced to endure a life of endless suffering will surely lead him or her to realize that worldly life yields little—if any—real satisfaction or happiness, and that it is necessary to seek it in something Higher, in the Quest of the true Spiritual Life, or in God. Somewhere, sometime, this need will call forth an answer.

❖ ❖ ❖

Why should anyone reject physicians and their medicines for osteopaths and their manipulations, or both for healers and their prayers? The power which cures works through all three; if it did not, if it worked through a single channel alone, the others would never have been needed, found, and used.

* * *

In the moment when you feel that actual contact with the One Infinite Life-Power has been made, draw it into the body and let it permeate every part, every organ, and every atom. It will tend to dissolve sickness and drive out disease.

* * *

Some of the thoughts which poison mind and blood, negatives to be cast out and kept out, are: spite, ill will, unforgiveness, violent conduct, and constant fault-finding.

* * *

Metaphysical or faith cure is an oversimplification of the healing problem and consequently yields only a part-truth. Bodily healing is an occasional by-product of the healing of thought and feeling or the re-education of moral chacter; it is not at all the invariable result of such processes. Sickness may come to advanced students for a variety of causes, some of which arise from outside the individual. Karma is the commonest, but one such cause might be the application of a test or ordeal from the divine soul to the human ego that aspires to evolve more rapidly.

To pray for a bodily cure and nothing more is a limited and limiting procedure. Pray also to be enlightened as to why this sickness fell upon you. Ask also what you can do to remove its cause. And above all, ask for the Water of Life, as Jesus bade the woman at the well to ask.

5

DEATH AND SEPARATION

When the end of life comes, and you go out of it like a candle in the wind, what then happens depends upon your character, your prevailing consciousness, your preparedness, and your last thoughts.

* * *

One who has had the good fortune to have a loving companion in marriage should not rail at Destiny when this helpmate is taken away. The same karma which brought the two together has also severed the relationship. But this is only temporary. There is really no loss, as mind speaks to mind in silent moments. Love and companionship of high quality will act as an attractive force to bring them together again somewhere, sometime. Many feel this in the inner understanding.

* * *

Why some are taken away by death at a young age and with a lovely soul is one of those mysteries which we must leave unexplained with the laws of destiny and recompense. Despite the natural feeling of being grievously wounded, the bereaved person should resign in trust to the will of God and in faith that the departed will be taken care of wherever he or she is by the Father of us all.

* * *

The passing away of a loved one and what the personal loss means to the bereaved is, of course, beyond the reach of any external comment which can be made. Words seem cold and useless at such times; all one can do is to accept, and humbly resign oneself to, the Higher Will.

Although it is painful to lose our loved ones, this is often the only way by which we learn of our deep need to form some inner detachment, as well as the unalterable fact that worldly life is inseparable from suffering. Such bitter lessons are instructive; they make us aware that we must turn to the spiritual Quest if we are to find contentment and enduring happiness.

The passing away of a loved one is a heavy blow—one for which most people are improperly prepared, because they are not yet willing to face the inescapable fact that all life is stamped with transiency and loss and sorrow. Only by seeking refuge in the immortality of the Overself and in discovering the truth and wisdom of the Divine Purpose, can we also learn how to endure the suffering on the ever-changing face of life. "Letting go" is the hardest of all lessons to learn; yet it is the most necessary for spiritual advancement.

Sympathy and understanding go to those who have endured the passing beyond of someone precious to them. Healing will, however, come in time. Those who are thus suffering should resign themselves to the will of Destiny and believe that the loved one is living still, and will return.

* * *

The process of dying is one to study. It is full of significance. So many things and interests to which the dying person has been attached are now to be left behind, so many persons to whom he or she has been tied with bonds of affection or repelled by feelings of dislike are about to disappear.

* * *

A dying person should cross the arms over the chest with interlaced fingers. He or she should withdraw the mind from everything earthly and raise it lovingly in the highest aspiration.

* * *

I have witnessed some advanced souls going through the process of passing to another sphere of consciousness, the process we call death, who spread mental sunshine around so that the bereaved ones gathered at the bedside felt it as a consoling counterbalance to their natural human grief. The truth made some kind of impression upon them that this universal event in Nature can actually be a change to brighter, happier, and freer existence.

* * *

When the time for exit from this world-scene duly comes, approach it with trust—feeling that the power which supported you in previous crises will not desert you now.

✠ ✠ ✠

A time comes when the prudent person, feeling intuitively or knowing medically that he or she has entered the last months or years of life, ought to prepare for death. Clearly an increasing withdrawal from worldly life is called for. Its activities, desires, attachments, and pleasures must give way more and more to repentance, worship, prayer, asceticism, and spiritual recollectedness. It is time to come home.

✠ ✠ ✠

We may deplore our foolish behaviour in life, our stupid errors or our fleshly weaknesses, but in those moments of dying we have the chance to die in wisdom and in peace. Yes, it is a chance given to us, but we have to take it by keeping our sight fixed on the highest that we know.

✠ ✠ ✠

Death can open out higher possibilities to the man or woman who leaves this existence in faith, who trusts the Overself and commits themself to its leading without clinging to the body which is being left.

✠ ✠ ✠

I would like to die as peaceably as Lu Hsian-Shan, the Chinese mentalist philosopher. One evening he knew his hour had come, so he bathed, put on clean clothes, sat down and remained in silent meditation until he passed away seventeen hours later.

✤ ✤ ✤

The best way to minister to a dying person depends on various factors: each situation is different and individual. In general it may be suggested that the first thing is not to panic but to remain calm. The next is to look inwardly for one's own highest reference-point. The third is then to turn the person over to the Higher Power. Finally, and physically, one may utter a prayer aloud, or chant a mantram on his or her behalf—some statement indicating that the happening is more a homecoming than a homeleaving.

✤ ✤ ✤

When suffering reaches its zenith or frustration is drawn out too long, when the heart is resigned to hopelessness or the mind to apathy, people often say that they do not wish to live any more and that they await the coming of death. They think only of the body's death, however. This will not solve their problem, for the same situation—under another guise—will repeat itself in a later birth. The only real solution is to seek out the inner reality of their longing for death. They want it because they believe it will separate them from their problems and disappointments. *But these are the ego's burdens.* Therefore the radical separation from them is achievable only by separating permanently from the ego itself. Peace will then come—and come forever.

✤ ✤ ✤

Why become resentful and bitter at the loss? Why

not be grateful at having had the good fortune at all, and for possessing memory of it that cannot be lost? Why not regard it as enough to have experienced such happiness, even for a little time, when in the chances of life it could have passed you by altogether? Why not receive the gifts of destiny humbly without trying to own them with a tight vampire-like grip?

✤ ✤ ✤

So long as you listen to your little ego alone, and let the voice of the Overself remain unheard and unknown, so long will all your cunning and your caution avail you little in the end when the body has to be left and the mind must return to its own proper sphere.

✤ ✤ ✤

The only way to receive trustworthy contact with the spirit of a departed loved one is by prayer and silence, practised at the same time every night. There may only be a sense of the other's presence, or there may be a clear message imparted, possibly, in a dream. Patience is needed. Moreover, this cannot be repeated more than a few times.

✤ ✤ ✤

We who find ourselves in old age with brittle bones and shrunken flesh, with wrinkled face and greyed hair, may find this a depressing experience. But like every other situation in life there is another way to look at it—perhaps in compensation for what we suffer. And that is to sum up the lessons of a lifetime and prepare ourselves for the next incarnation so that we shall better perform the necessary work on ourselves when that comes.

✠ ✠ ✠

There is a part of oneself which cannot die, cannot pass into annihilation. But it is very deep down. The sage encounters it before bodily death and learns to establish his or her consciousness therein. The others encounter it during some phase in the after-death state.

✠ ✠ ✠

This dismal fact is the mark on all things, and creatures: that they pass away, have a transient existence, and in this absolute sense lack reality. They appear for awhile, seem substantial and eventful, but are in truth prolonged mirages. If this were all the story it would be melancholy enough. But it is not. *That* whence they came, to which they go back, does not pass away. That is the Real, that is the Consciousness which gave the universe, of which *we* are a part, its existence. Out of that stems this little flower in each life which is the best, highest self. If we search for it and discover it, we recover our origin, return to our source, and *as such* do not pass away. Yes, the forms are lost in the end but the being within them is not.

6

FINDING A BROADER PERSPECTIVE

The effect of a full and proper absorption of these ideas is to strengthen you and invigorate your purpose, to make you feel that what is behind the universe is behind you too.

If you identify with the little ego *alone,* you may believe and feel that you have to solve your problems *alone.* In that case, the burden will be heavier than it need be. But if you recognize that this planet has its own governor, the World-Mind, you need not feel forlorn, since you are included in the world.

❖ ❖ ❖

There is a universal order, a way which Nature (God) has of arranging things. This is why what we see around us as the world expresses all-pervading meaning, intelligence, and purpose. But we catch only a mere hint of these veiled qualities—the mystery which recedes from them is immeasurably greater.

❖ ❖ ❖

The universe is perfect because God is perfect. But it is for each of us to find and see this perfection for ourself, otherwise the trouble and tragedy in life may obstruct one's vision and obscure one's path.

❖ ❖ ❖

Whatever happens in the world around you, so train your thoughts and feelings as to keep your knowledge of the World-Idea, and your vision of its harmony, ever with you.

❖ ❖ ❖

Do your best to mend matters, the best you can,

then leave the results to destiny and the Overself. You can't do more anyway. You can modify your destiny, but certain events are unchangeable because the world is not yours but God's. You may not know at first what events these are, therefore you must act intelligently and intuitively: later you can find out and accept. Whatever happens, the Overself is still there and will bring you through and out of your troubles. Whatever happens to your material affairs happens to your body, not the real YOU. The hardest part is when you have others dependent on you. Even then you must learn how to commend them to the kindly care of the Overself, and not try to carry all the burden on your own shoulders. If it can take care of you, it can take care of them, too.

Philosophy teaches us a wiser course than mere fatalism, a truer one than mere faith in free will. It teaches us that even when the stars in the firmament appear to work against us, the stars of worthy ideals will always work for us. It liberates us from anxieties about our horoscope because it gives us certitudes that the right causes we set going must have right effects. It gives our life's ship sails and rudder, port and map; we need not drift.

That our mortal destiny is made up of welcome and unwelcome circumstances or happenings is a certainty. There is no human being whose pattern fails to be so chequered—only the black and white squares are unequal in number, and the proportion differs from one person to another. It hurts to confess this duality of pain with joy, this temporality which threatens every happiness; but this truth is unassailable, as Buddha knew and taught.

There are tides of fortune and circumstances whose ebb and flow wash the lives of humankind. There are cycles of changes which must be heeded and with which our plans and activities must be harmonized, if we are to live without friction and avoid wasting strength in futile struggles. We must learn when to move forward and thus rise to the crest of the tide, and when to retreat and retire.

We must find the faith and some of us even the certitude that if it had been possible to think a better cosmos into being, the World-Mind's infinite wisdom would have done so. We cannot believe in God without accepting God's universe also.

We may freely leave the future to our stars, if we know that we can be true to ourselves.

It is pardonable to wish a change of situation when it is grievous but it is better to enquire first what message the situation holds for us. Otherwise we may be attempting to elude the Overself's directive and thereby incurring the danger of an even greater disaster.

❖ ❖ ❖

With this serene acceptance of Life, this glad co-operation with it and willing obedience to its laws, you begin to find that henceforth Life is for you. Events begin to happen, circumstances so arrange themselves, and contacts so develop themselves that what you really need for your further development or expression appears of its own accord.

❖ ❖ ❖

While people are not yet ready for the conscious and deliberate development of their spiritual life, they must submit to its unconscious and compulsive development by the forces of Nature.

❖ ❖ ❖

When one's personal life is miraculously saved during some period of great danger, perhaps in the face of death, it is for a purpose.

❖ ❖ ❖

Keep your inner shrine within the heart reserved for the Ideal. Worship there the Spirit that is birthless and deathless, indestructible and divine. Life in this world is like foam on the sea: it passes all to soon; but the moments given in adoration and obeisance to the Soul count for eternal gain. The most tremendous historic happenings on this earth are, after all, only pictures that pass through consciousness like a dream. Once you awaken to the Real, you see them for what they are. Then you will live in Its serenity, and it will no longer matter if the pictures themselves are stormy and agitated. It is the greatest good fortune to attain such serenity—to be lifted above passion and hatred, prejudice and fear, greed and discontent, and yet to be able to attend effectively and capably to one's worldly duties. It is possible to reach this state. You may have had glimpses of it already. Someday, sometime, if you are patient, you will enter it to stay—and the unimaginably rewarding and perfect purpose of your life, of all your lifetimes, will be fulfilled.

It is in the very nature of things that the good should ultimately triumph over the bad, that the true should dissolve the false. This understanding should bring you patience.

From the ultimate point of view there are no sins, only ignorance; there are no clumsy falls, only steps forward to the heart's wiser levels; there are no misfortunes, only lessons in the art of disentanglement.

❖ ❖ ❖

Think of yourself as the individual and you are sure to die; think of yourself as the universal and you enter deathlessness, for the universal is always and eternally there. We know no beginning and no ending to the cosmic process. Its being IS: we can say no more. Be that rather than this—that which is as infinite and homeless as space, that which is timeless and unbroken. Take the whole of life as your own being. Do not divorce, do not separate yourself from it. It is the hardest of tasks for it demands that we see our own relative insignificance amid this infinite and vast process. The change that is needed is entirely a mental one. Change your outlook and with it "heaven will be added unto you."

❖ ❖ ❖

These eternal truths must be brought down into your simple daily experience. Every act is to be done in their light, every thought held in their atmosphere.

❖ ❖ ❖

The philosophic attitude is to be in the world but not of it, to hold necessary useful or beautiful possessions but not to be held by them. It knows the transiency of things, the brevity of pleasures, the movement of every situation. This is the way of the universe, the ebb and flow of life, the power of time to alter the pattern of every existence. So the philosopher adjusts to this rhythm, learns how and when to let go and when to hold on, and so retains inner equilibrium, inner poise and peace. During stormy times the philosopher stands firm as a rock, studies their meaning and accepts their lesson; during sunny times he or she avoids identifying with the little ego and remembers that one's true security is in the Overself.

✠ ✠ ✠

The constant practice of identifying yourself with the mind rather than with the body-idea which inheres in it, leads in time to a certain freeing of yourself from yourself.

✠ ✠ ✠

Who does not know the healing powers of time, which ends the memory of sorrow and the feeling of pain?

✠ ✠ ✠

Life today is filled with too many cares or uncertainties for anyone in any part of the world to enjoy complete happiness.

✠ ✠ ✠

Metaphysically, every thing and every thought contains in itself the form of its opposite. We must try not to be attached to one opposite and not to be repelled by the other in a *personal* way. This does not mean that we may ignore them—indeed we cannot do so, for practical life requires that we attempt at least to negotiate them—but that we deal with them in an equable and impersonal way. Thus we keep free of the bonds of possessiveness. If we try to cling to one of the opposites alone whilst rejecting the other, we are doomed to frustration. To accept what is inherent in the nature of things is therefore a wise act. If, through being personally hurt by it, we are unwilling to do so, if we rebel against it, then we shall succeed only in hurting ourselves all the more. To run away from one of the opposites and to run after the other is an unwise act. We must find a balance between them; we must walk between the two extremes; we must ascend the terrace above the standpoint which affirms and above that which negates: for the entire truth is never caught by either and is often missed by both. For the way in which our consciousness works shuts us up, as it were, in a prison house of relativistic experiences which are the seeming real but never the actually real. To accept both and yet to transcend both, is to become a philosopher. To transcend the opposites we have to cease thinking about what effect they will have upon us personally. We have to drop the endless "I" reference which blinds us to the truth about them. We must refuse to set up our personal preferences as absolute standards, our relative standpoints as eternal ones. To do this is to cease worrying over events on the one hand, to cease grabbing at things on the other. It is indeed to rise to an impersonal point of view and enter into harmony with what Nature is seeking to do in us and in our environment. We have to find a new and higher set of values. For so long as we cling to a personal standpoint we are enslaved by time and emotion, whereas as soon as we drop it for the philosophic one, we are liberated into a serene timeless life.

✠ ✠ ✠

What is the practical value of the teaching about time? The full answer to this question would embrace many fields, but here is one of the most important. Philosophy teaches its students to apply the double point of view to the outward happenings of their own lives as it does to the inward contents of their sense-experience. From the ordinary point of view, the nature of an event determines whether it is a good or an evil one; from the philosophic point of view, the way you think about the event will determine whether it is good or evil for you. You should always put the two points of view together and never separate them, always balance the short-range one by the long-range one.

The higher point of view enables you to escape some of the suffering which the lower one would impose upon you. An event which to the worldly person seems staggeringly important and evil from the point of view of the moment, becomes smaller and smaller as the years recede and, consequently, less and less hurtful. Twenty years later it will have lost some of its power to shake you; fifty years later it will have lost still more—indeed, it may have lost so much as to cause you no further pain; one incarnation later it will not trouble you at all. When the student adopts the long-range point of view, he or she achieves the same result in advance and by anticipation of time. It is said that time heals all sorrows; if we seek the reason why, we shall find it is because it insensibly gives a more philosophic point of view to the sorrowful. The taste of water in a jar will be strongly sweetened by a cupful of sugar; the taste of water in a bucket will be moderately sweetened by it; the taste of water in a bathtub will be only slightly sweetened by it; and water in a lake will be apparently quite unmodified by it at all. In exactly the same way, the stream of happenings which makes up time for human consciousness gradually dilutes the suffering which each individual event may bring us.

The student is not content, however, to wait for such a slow process in order to reduce his or her suffering. By bringing the philosophic attitude to bear upon each event, as and when it occurs, you immediately reduce your suffering and fortify your peace. Every calamity which is seen from this standpoint becomes a means whereby you may ascend, if you will, to a higher level of understanding, a purer form of being. What you think about it and what you learn from it will be its real legacy to you. In his or her first fresh anguish the unawakened person may deny this; in the mental captivity which gives reality to the Present and drops it from the Past, he or she may see no meaning and no use in the calamity; but either by time or by philosophy you will one day be placed at the point of view where the significance of suffering will be revealed and where the necessity of suffering will be understood. This, indeed, is one of the great paradoxes of the human development: that suffering leads you step by step from the false self to the acceptance of the true self, and that the true self leads you step by step back to the acceptance of suffering.

If the worldly person agitatedly sees the event against the background of a moment, if the philosophic student calmly sees it against the background of an entire lifetime, the sage, while fully aware of both these points of view, offsets them altogether by adding a third one which does not depend on any dimension of time at all. From this third point of view, the sage sees both the event itself and the ego to whom it happens as illusory. He feels the sense of time and the sense of personality as unreal. Deep within his mind he holds unshakeably to the timeless character of true being, to the eternal life of the kingdom of heaven. In this mysterious state time cannot heal, for there are no wounds present whereof to be healed. So soon as we can take the reality out of time, so soon can we take the sting out of suffering. For the false self lives like a slave, bound to every passing sensation, whereas the true self lives in the timeless peace of the kingdom of heaven. As soon as we put ourselves into harmony with the true self, we put ourselves into harmony with the whole universe; we put ourselves beyond the reach of calamity. It may still happen, but it does not happen to nor is it felt by our real self. There is a sense of absolute security, a feeling that no harm can come to us. The philosophic student discovers the mission of time; it heals sorrows and, under karma or through evolution, cures evils. The sage solves the mystery of timelessness, which redeems humanity.

✽ ✽ ✽

When you have sufficiently purified your character, controlled your senses, developed your reason, and unfolded your intuition you are always ready to meet what comes and to meet it aright. You need not fear the future. Time is on your side. For you have stopped adding bad karma to your account and every fresh year adds good karma instead. And even where you must still bear the workings of the old adverse karma, you will still remain serene because you understand with Epictetus that "There is only one thing for which God has sent me into the world, and that is to perfect my nature in all sorts of virtue or strength; and there is nothing that I cannot use for that purpose." You know that each experience which comes to you is what you most need at the time, even though it be what you like least. You need it because it is in part nothing else than your own past thinking, feeling, and doing come back to confront you to enable you to see and study their results in a plain, concrete, unmistakable form. You make use of every situation to help your ultimate aims, even though it may hinder your immediate ones. Such serenity in the face of adversity must not be mistaken for supine fatalism or a lethargic acceptance of every untoward event as God's will. For although you will seek to understand why it has happened to you and master the lesson behind it, you will also seek to master the event itself and not be content to endure it helplessly. Thus, when all happenings become serviceable to you and when you know that your own reaction to them will be dictated by wisdom and virtue, the future can no more frighten you than the present can intimidate you. You cannot go amiss whatever happens. For you know too, whether it be a defeat or a sorrow in the world's eyes, whether it be a triumph or a joy, the experience will leave you better, wiser, and stronger than it found you, more prepared for the next one to come. The philosophic student knows that he or she is here to face, understand, and master precisely those events, conditions, and situations which others wish to flee and evade, that to make a detour around life's obstacles and to escape meeting its problems is, in the end, unprofitable. Such a student knows that wisdom must arise out of the fullness and not out of the poverty of experience and that it is no use non-cooperatively shirking the world's struggle, for it is largely through such struggle that one can bring forth his or her own latent resources. Philosophy does not refuse to face life, however tragic or however frightful it may be, and uses such experiences to profit its own higher purpose.

❖ ❖ ❖

But because we affirm that the powers of evil will destroy themselves in the end, this must not be mistaken to mean that we may all sit down in smug complacency. We ought not to make this an excuse for inaction. On the contrary, it should inspire us to stronger efforts to preserve the noblest things in life from their attack.

❖ ❖ ❖

Truth and love will conquer in the end—however far off that be—for they are deeply buried in the hearts of all people and will be slowly uncovered by the instruction which life itself gives. We must acquire something of God's patience.